Ente und Gans

Malbuch

Coloring Pages for Kids

Coloring Pages for Kids
An imprint of Ciparum LLC

Ente und Gans Malbuch
© 2017 Ciparum LLC
All rights reserved.
ISBN-10:1-63589-475-1
ISBN-13:978-1-63589-475-2

Coloring Pages for Kids

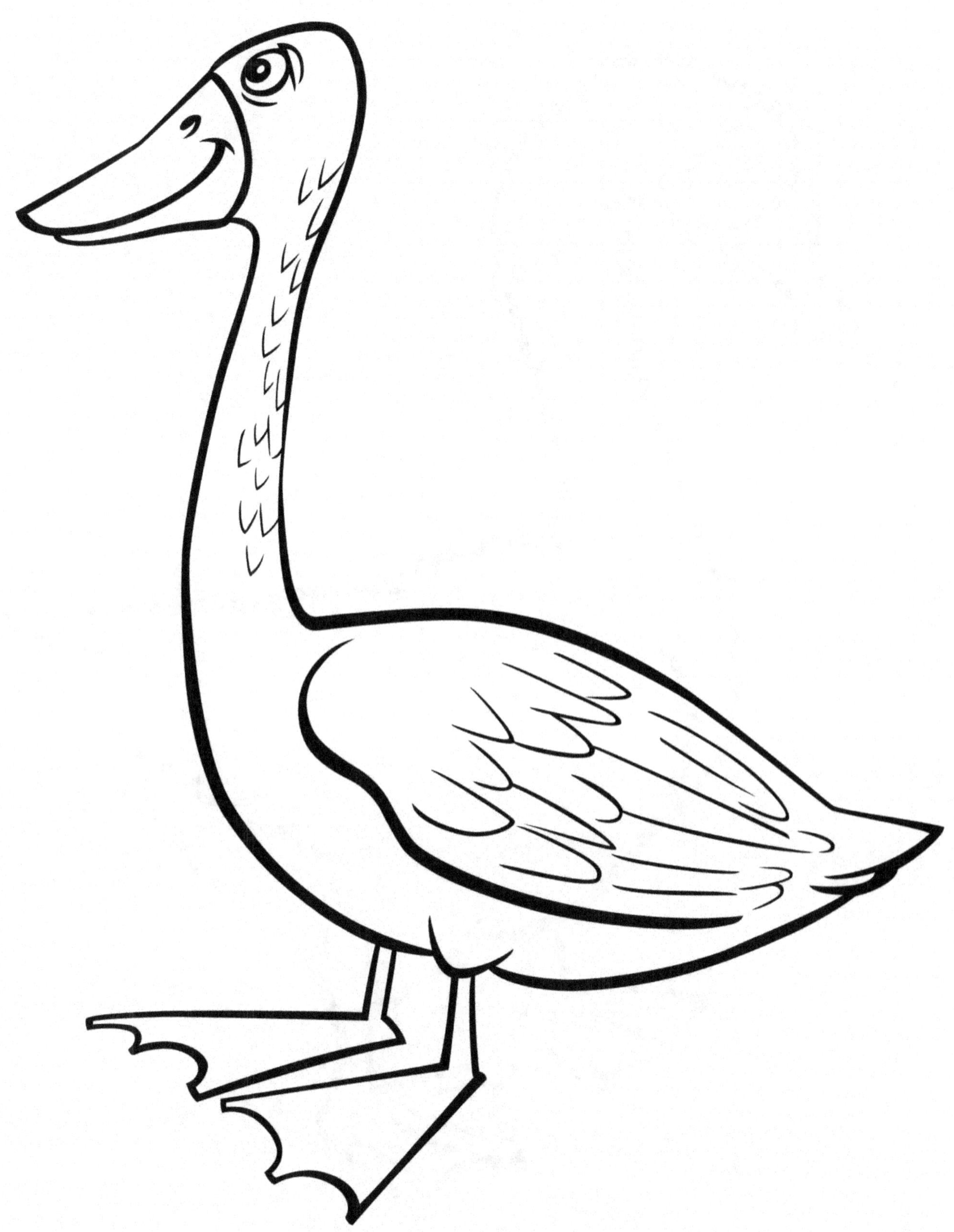

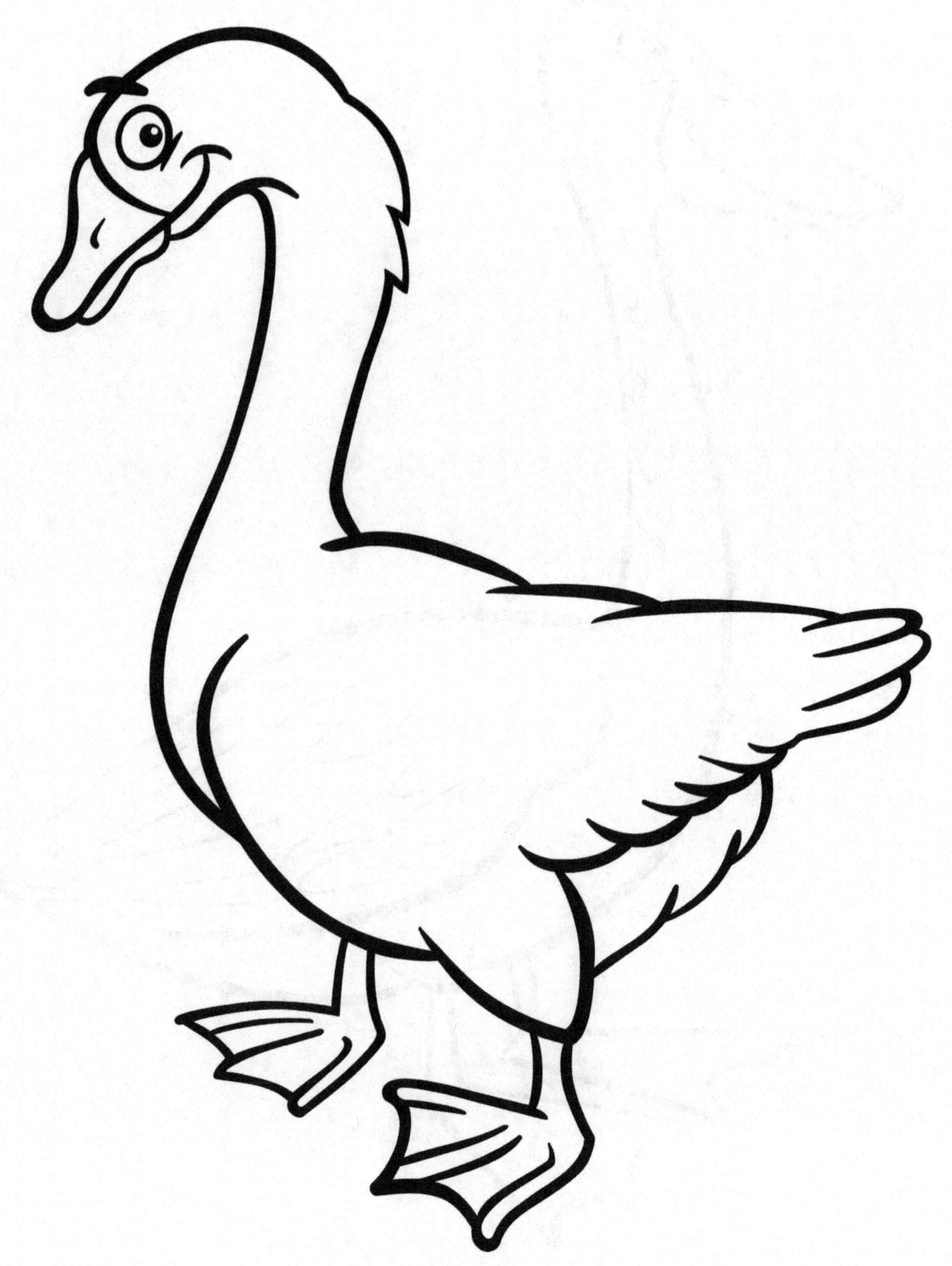

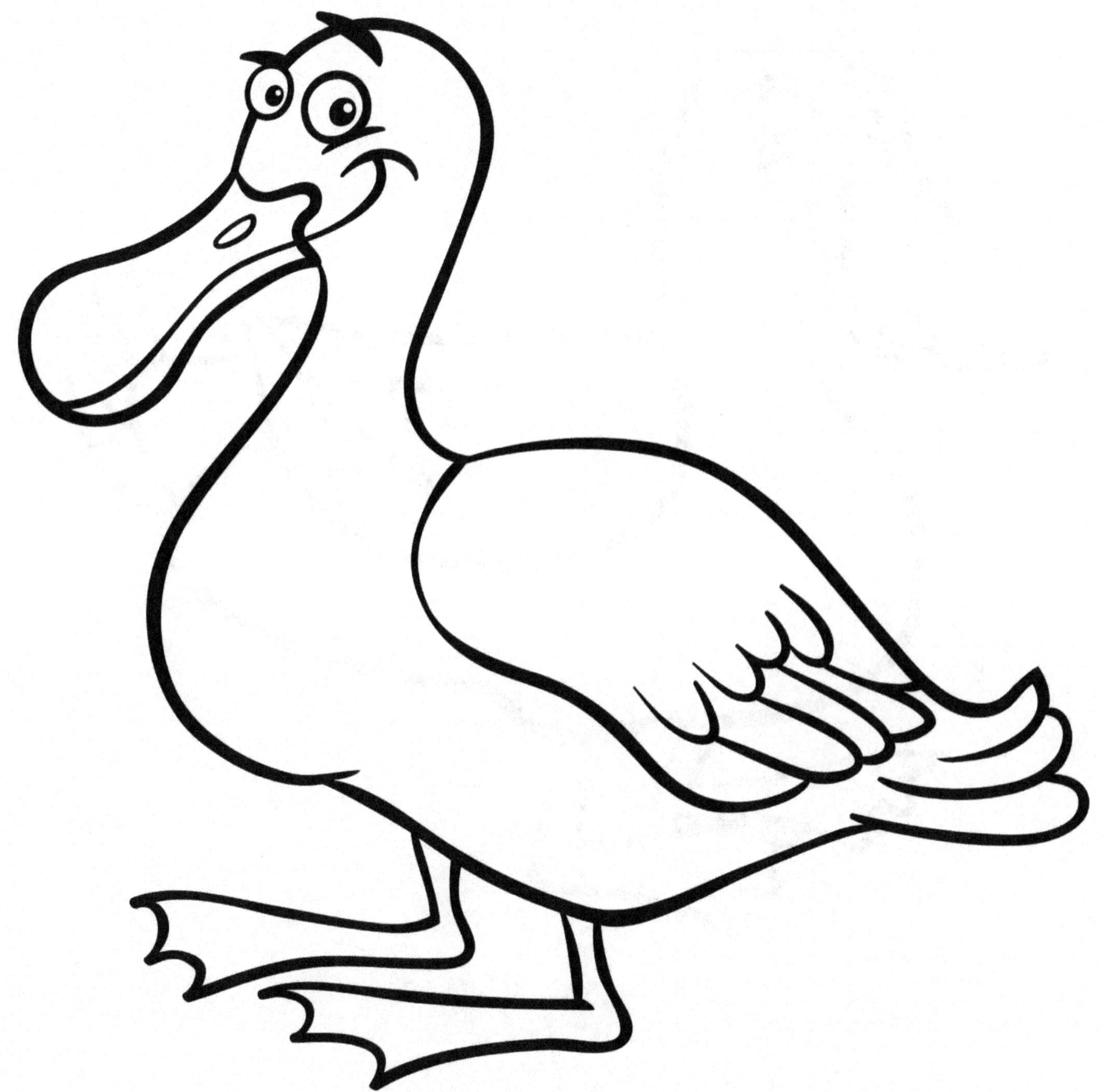

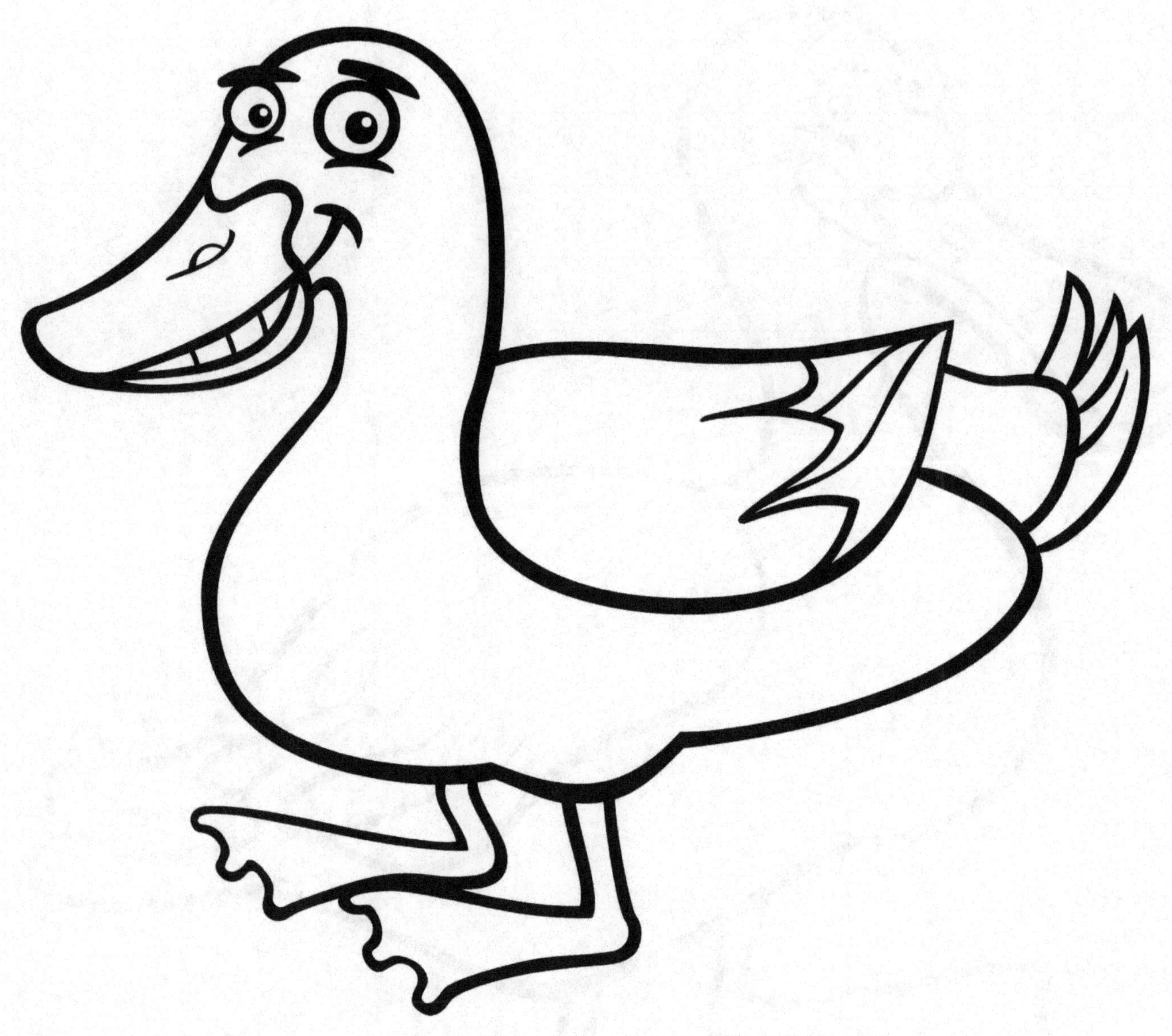

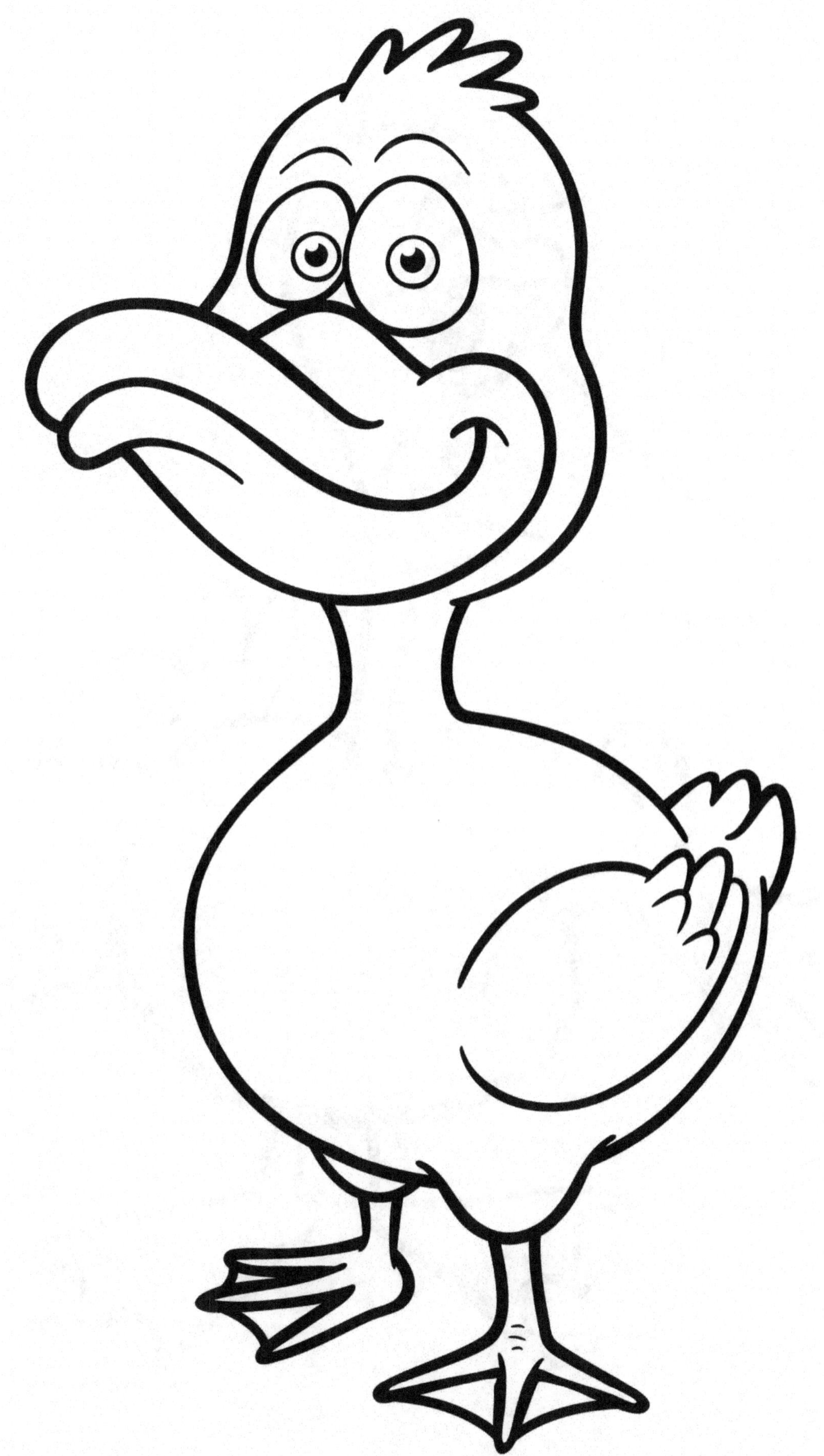

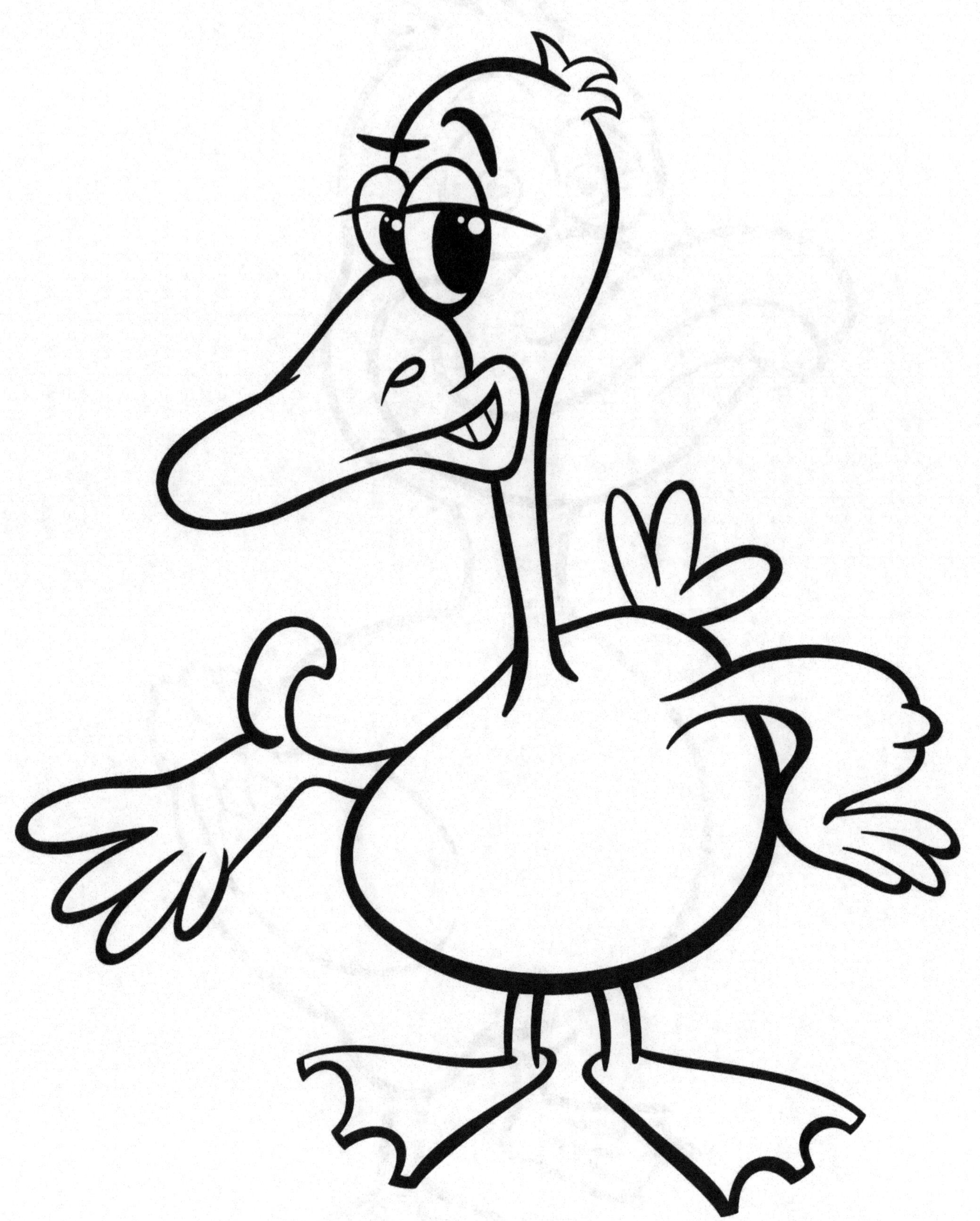

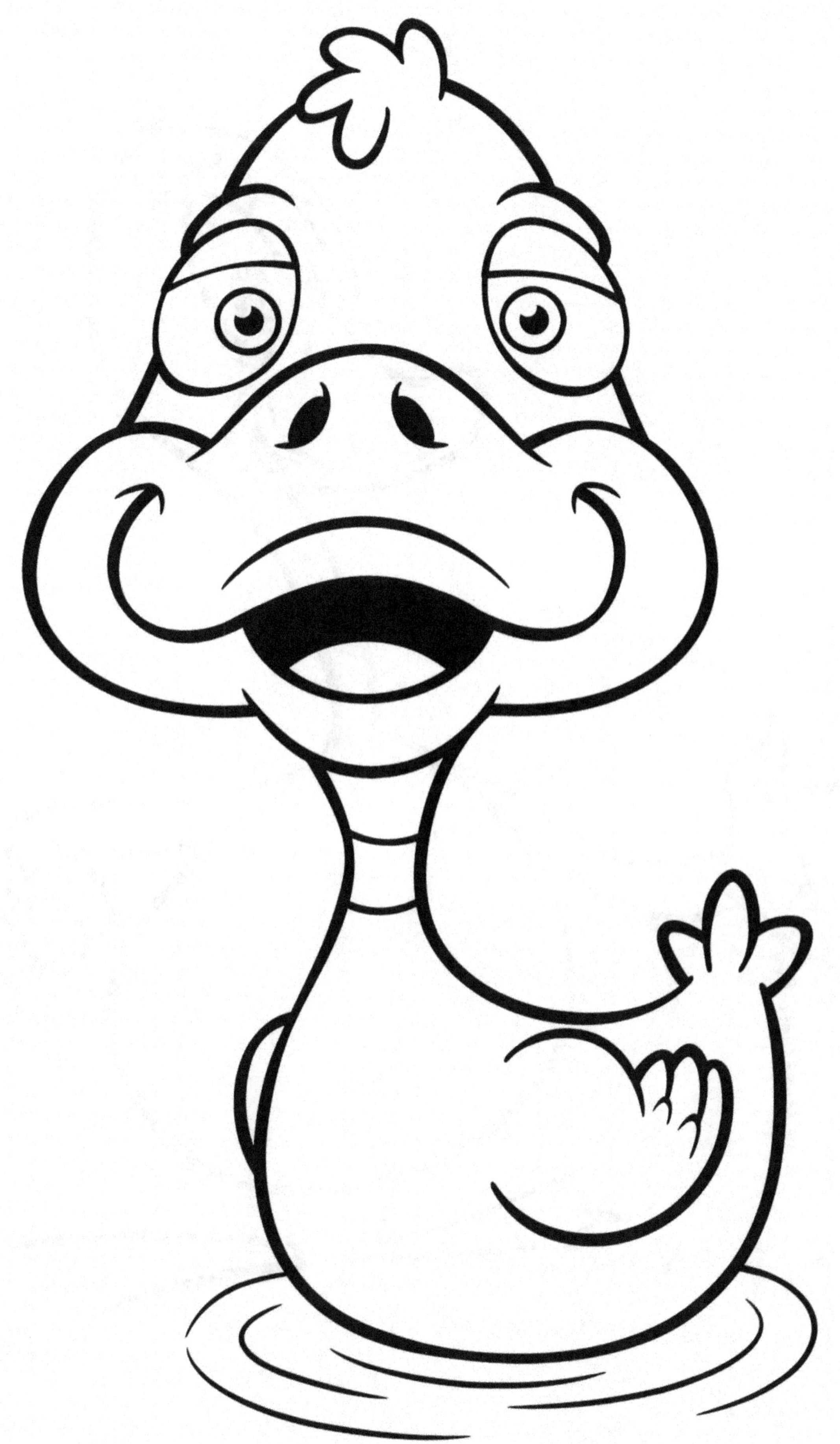

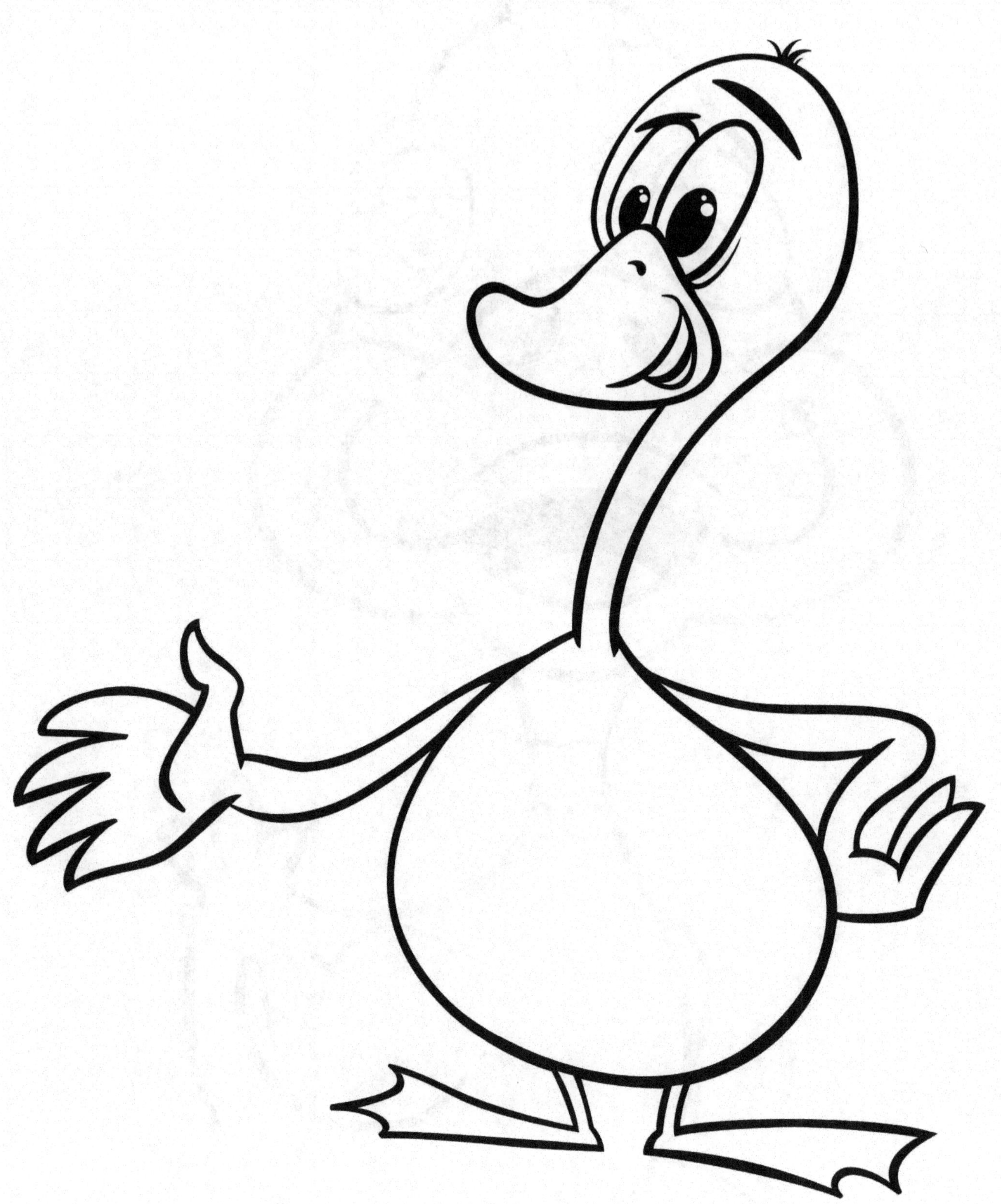

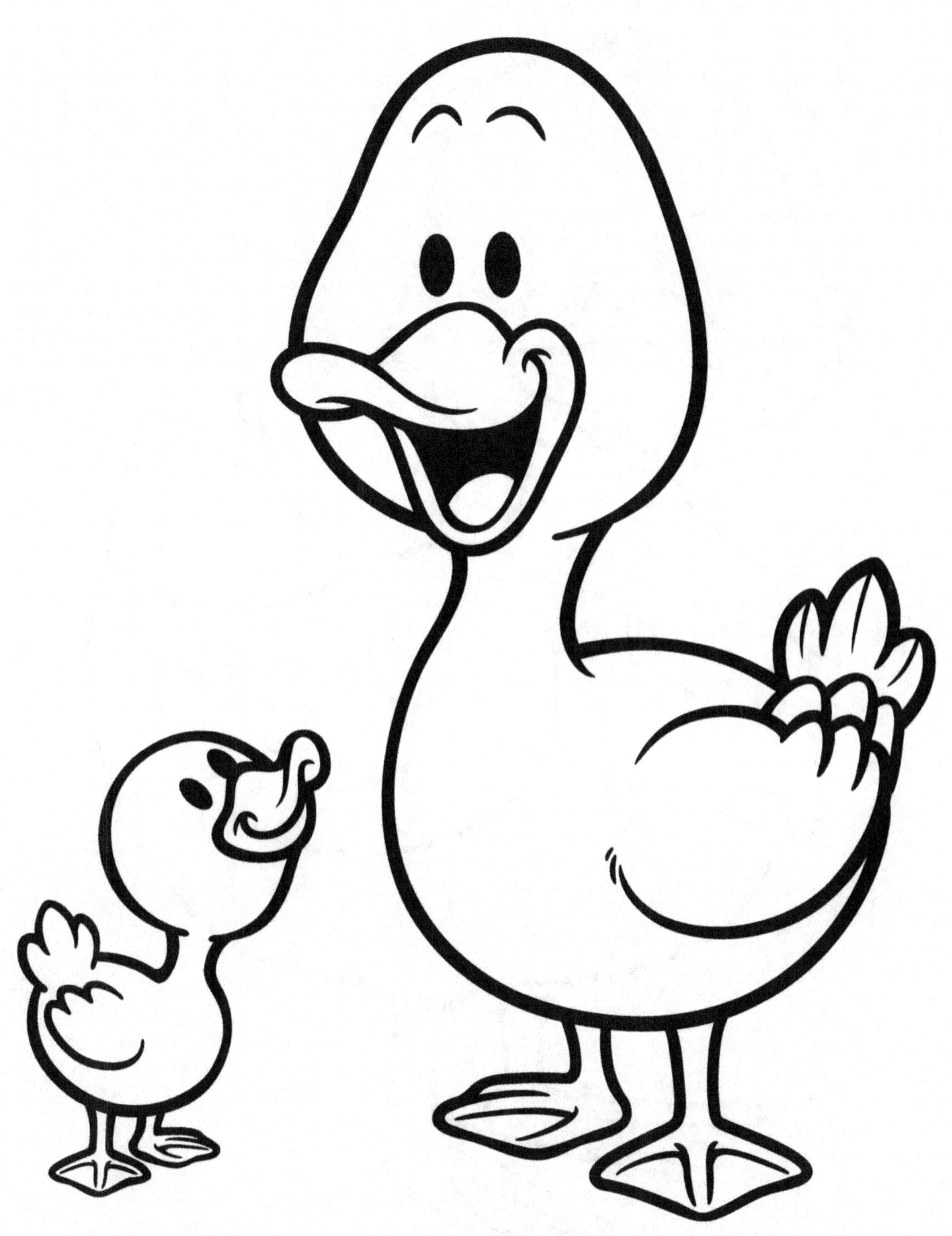

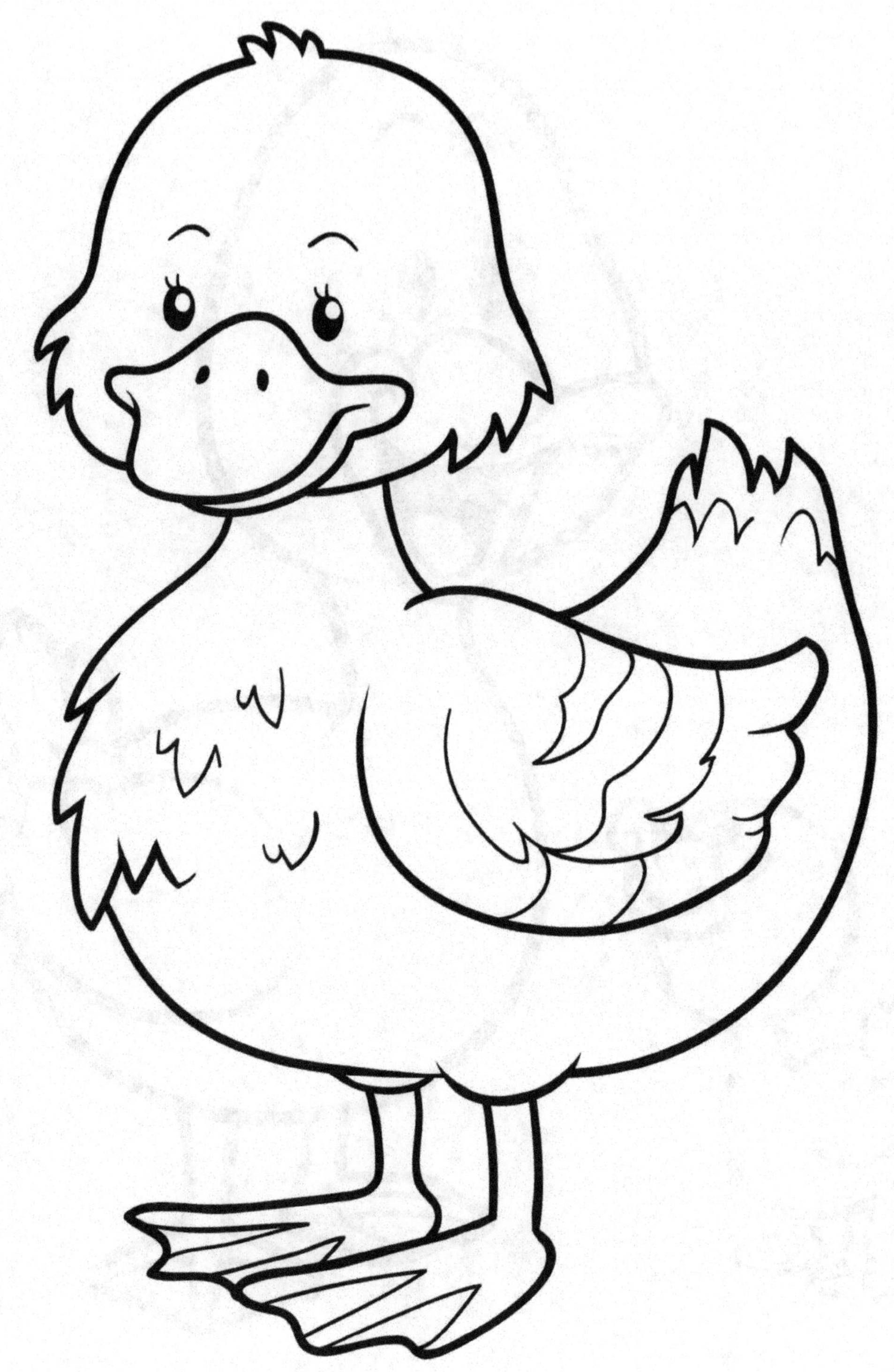

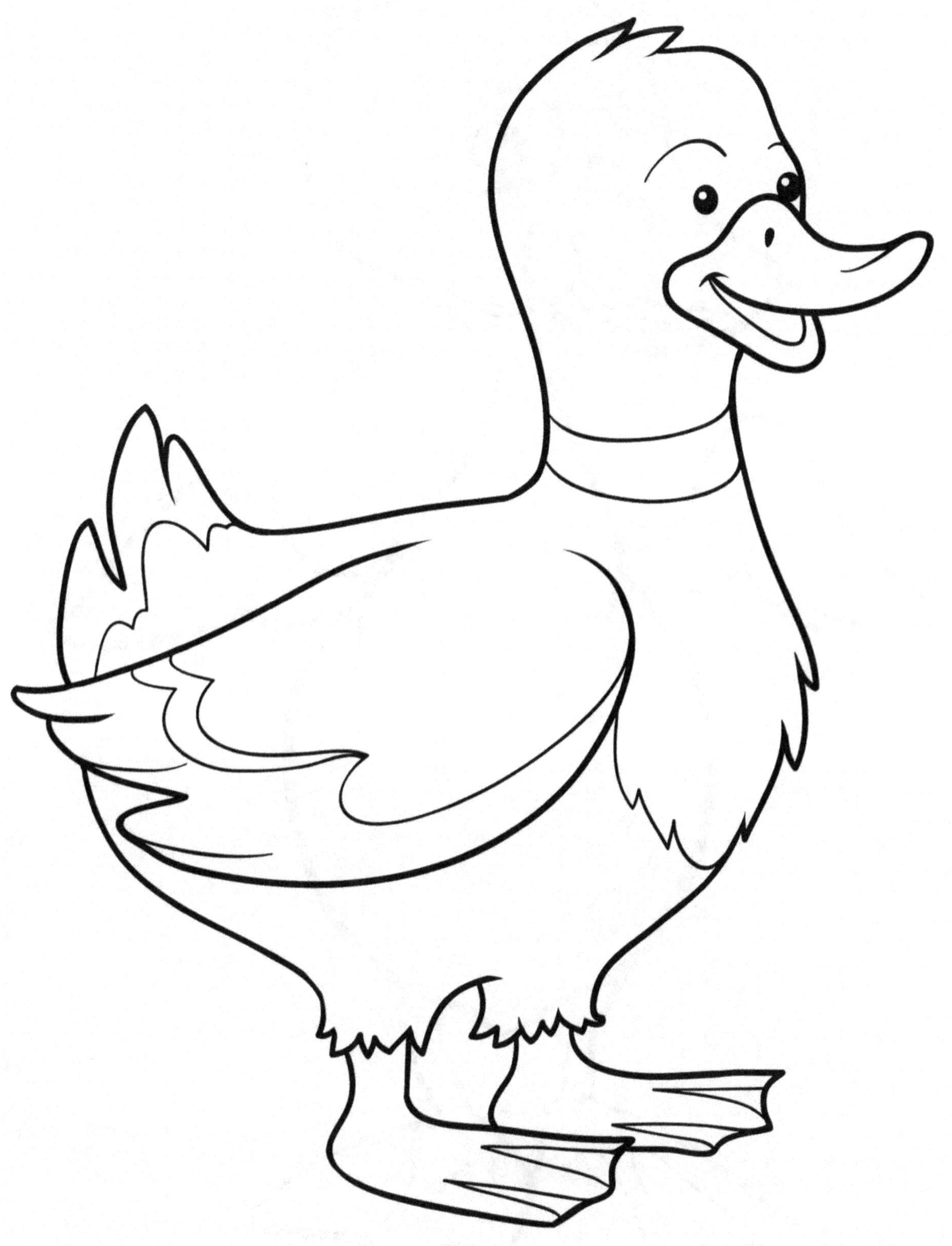

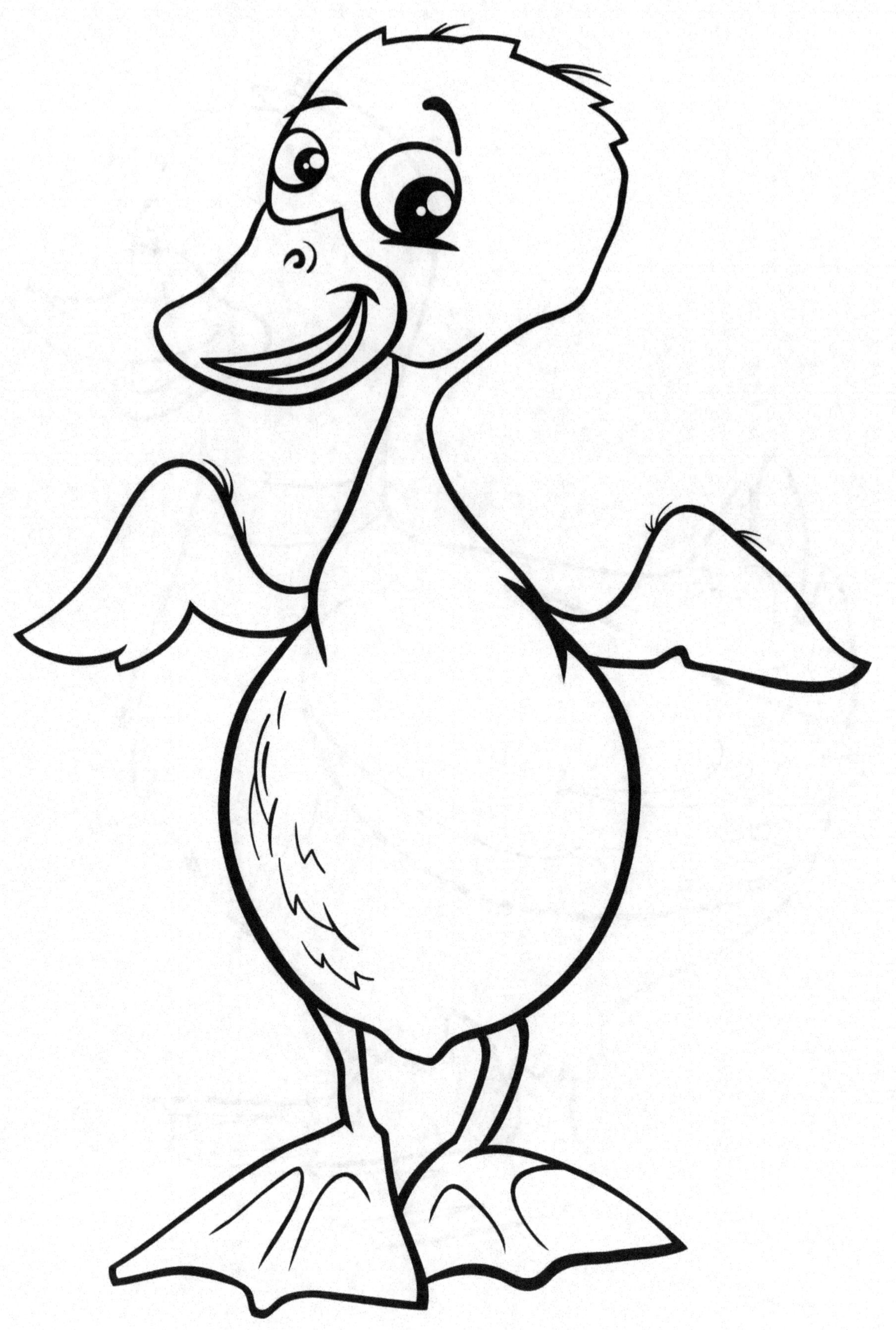

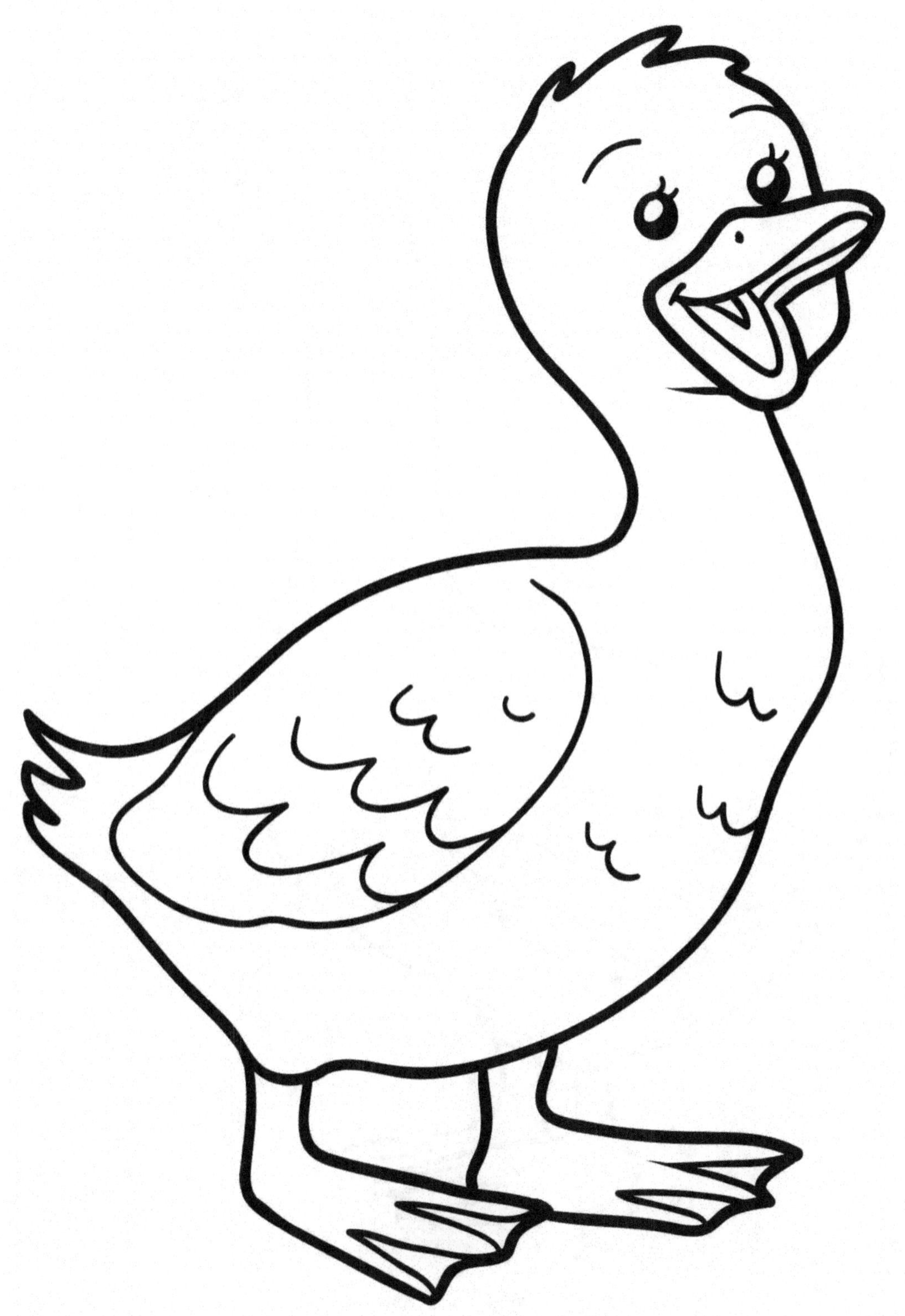

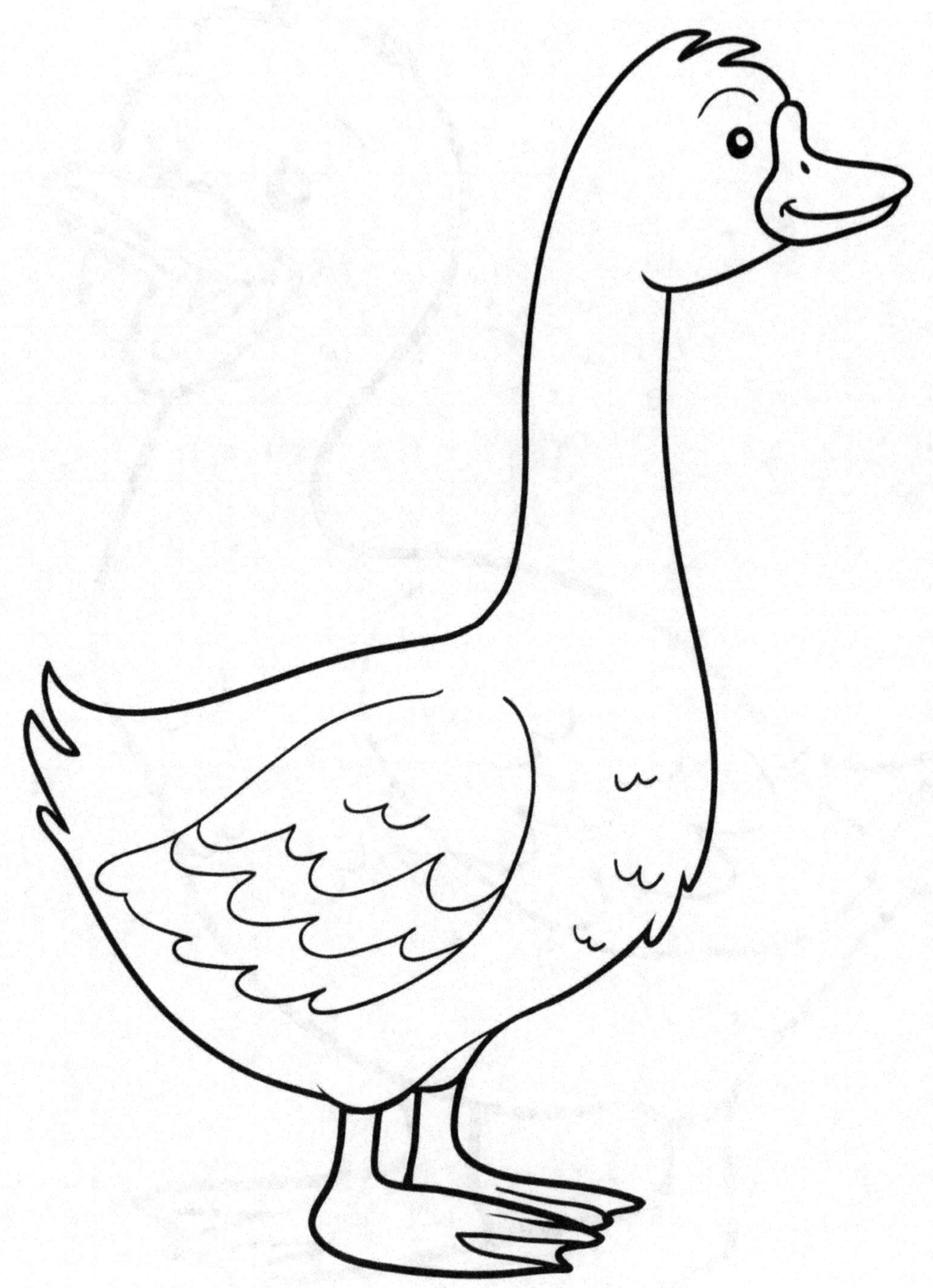

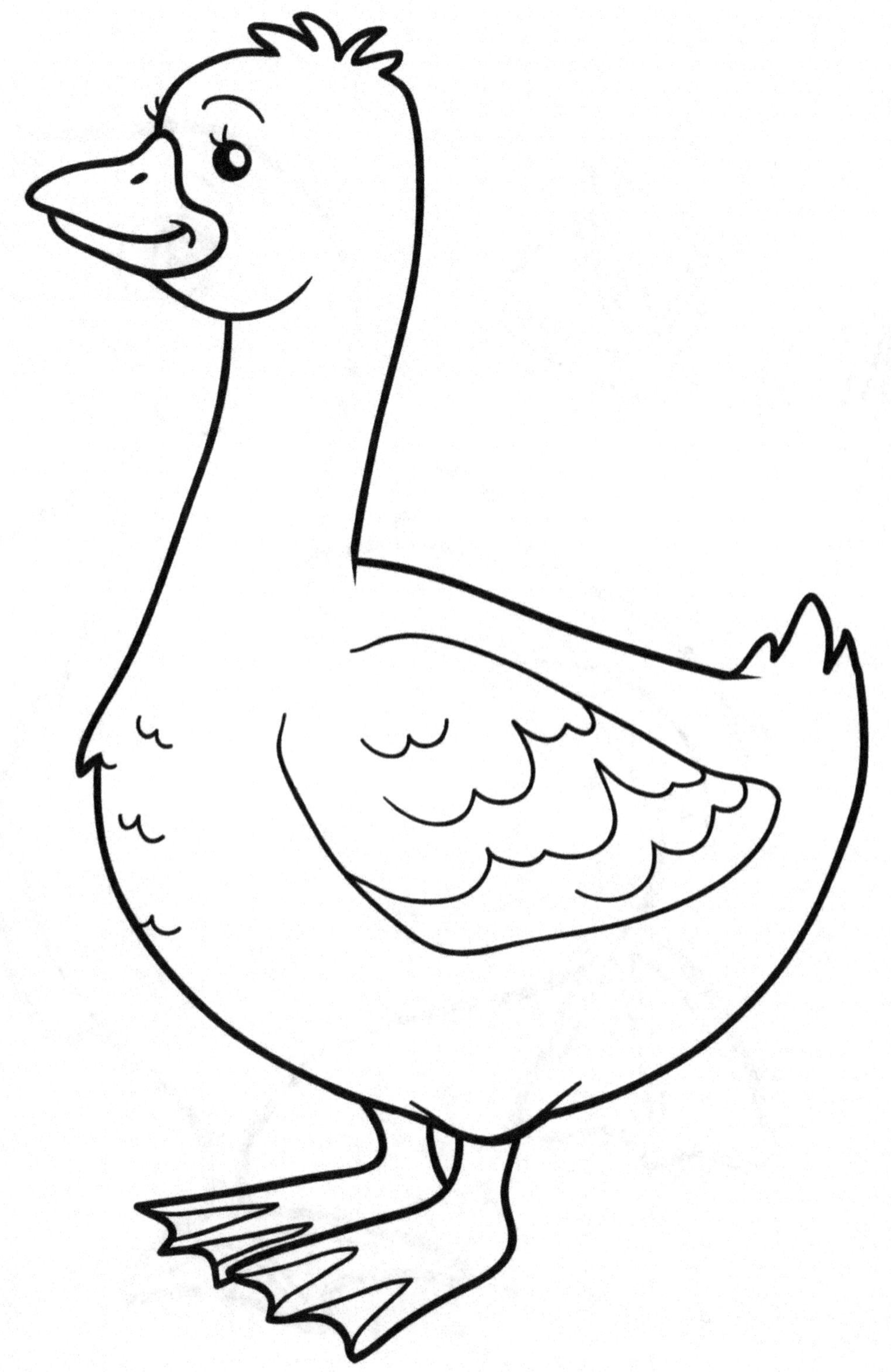

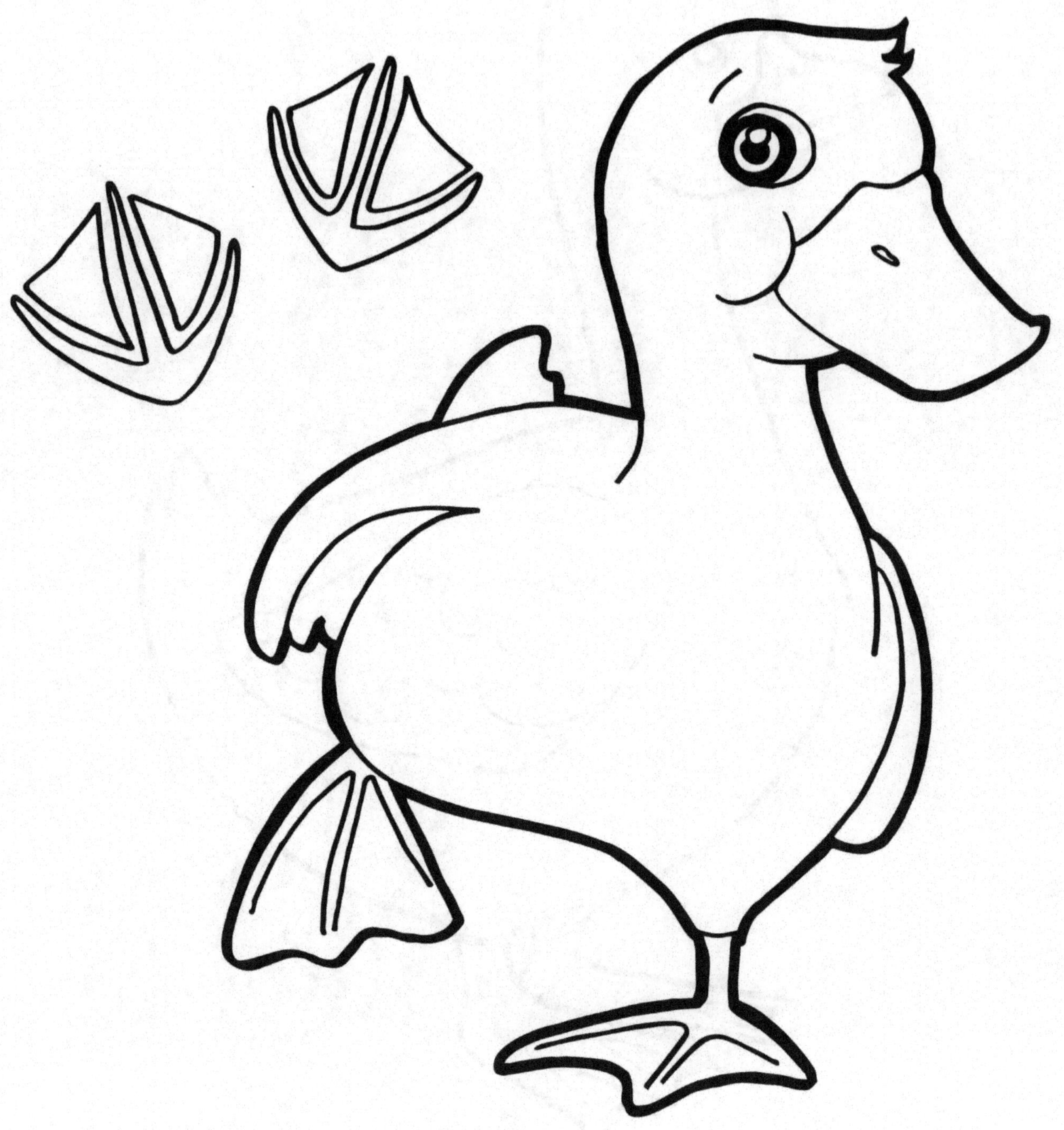

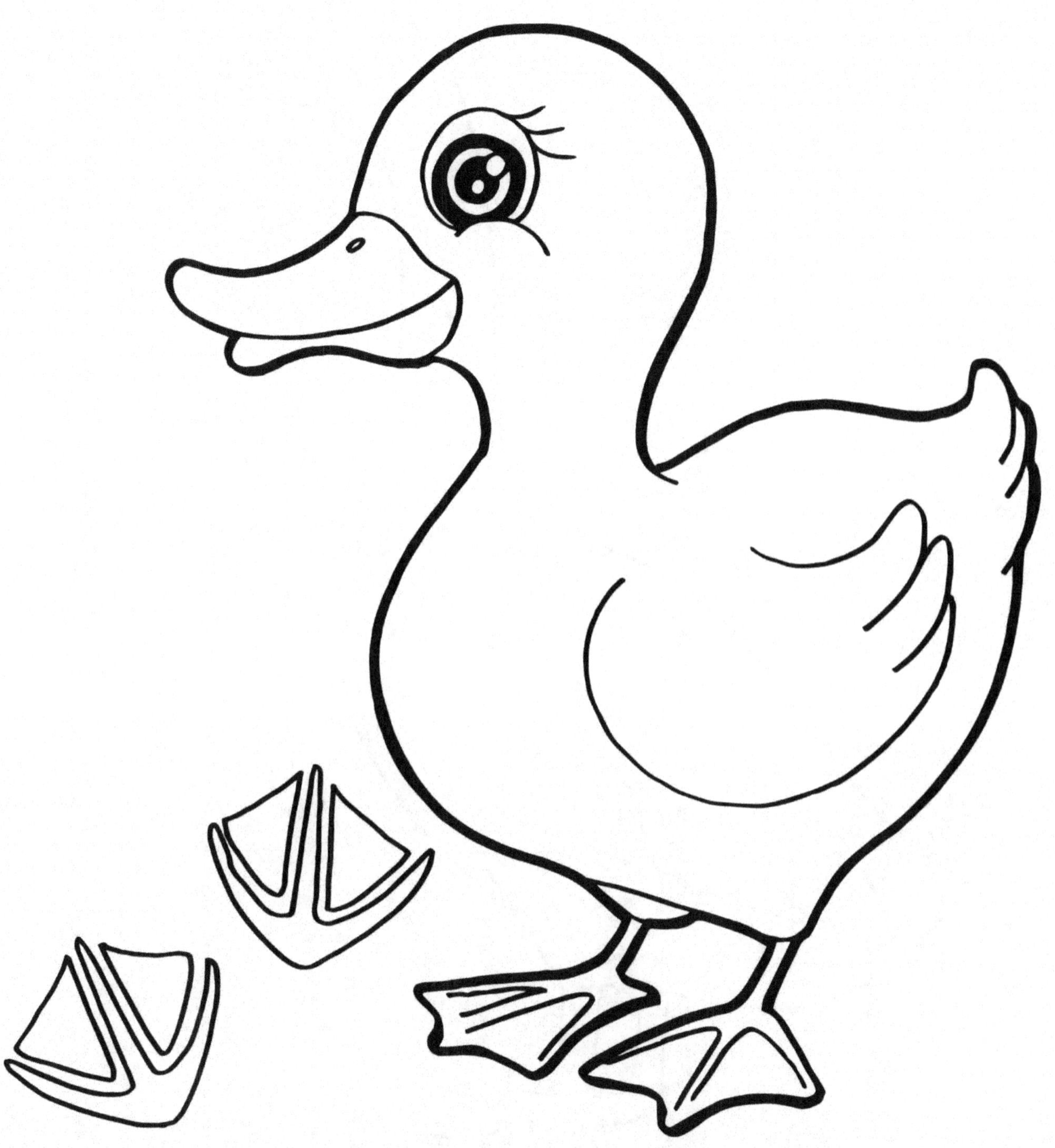

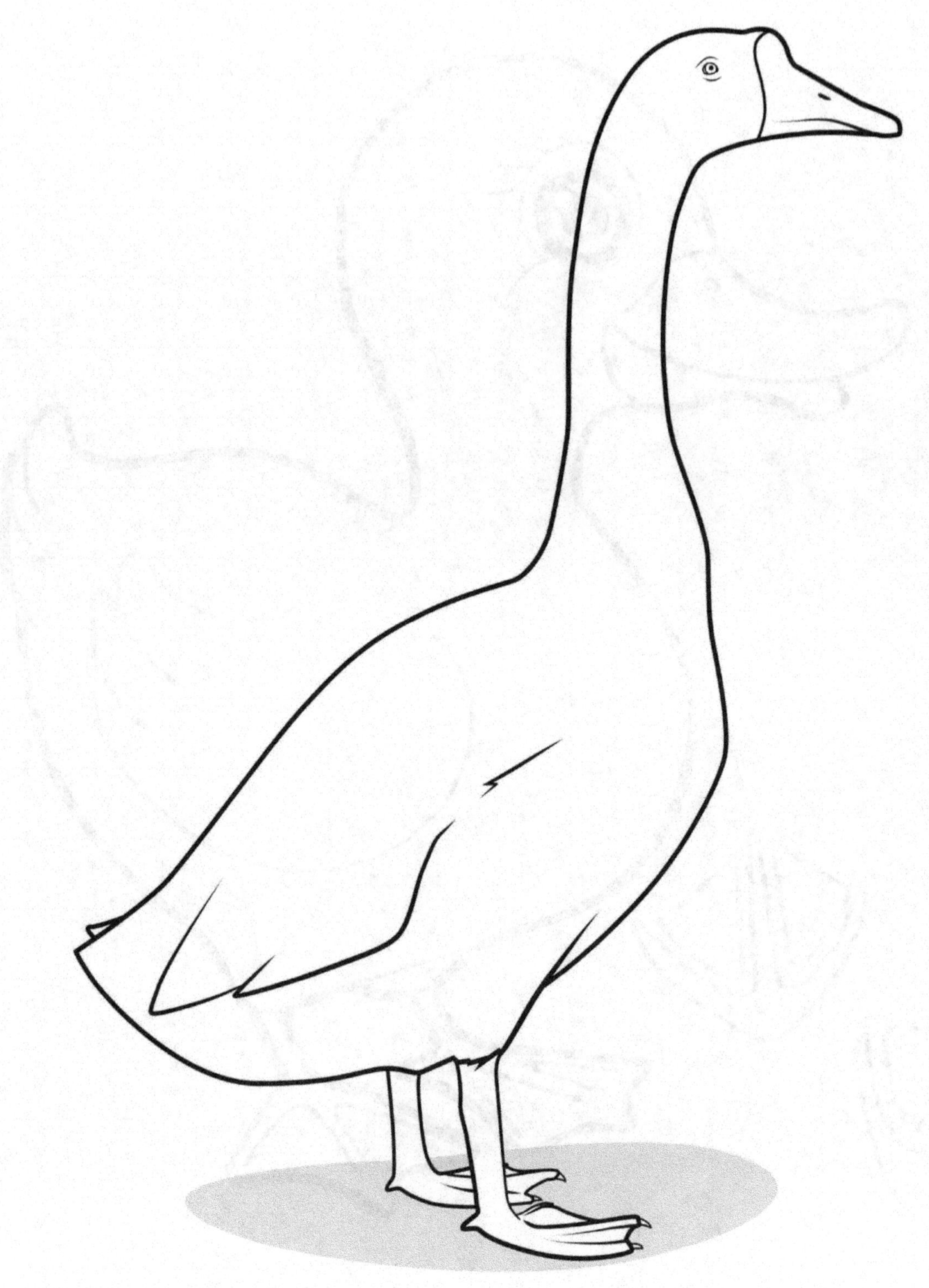

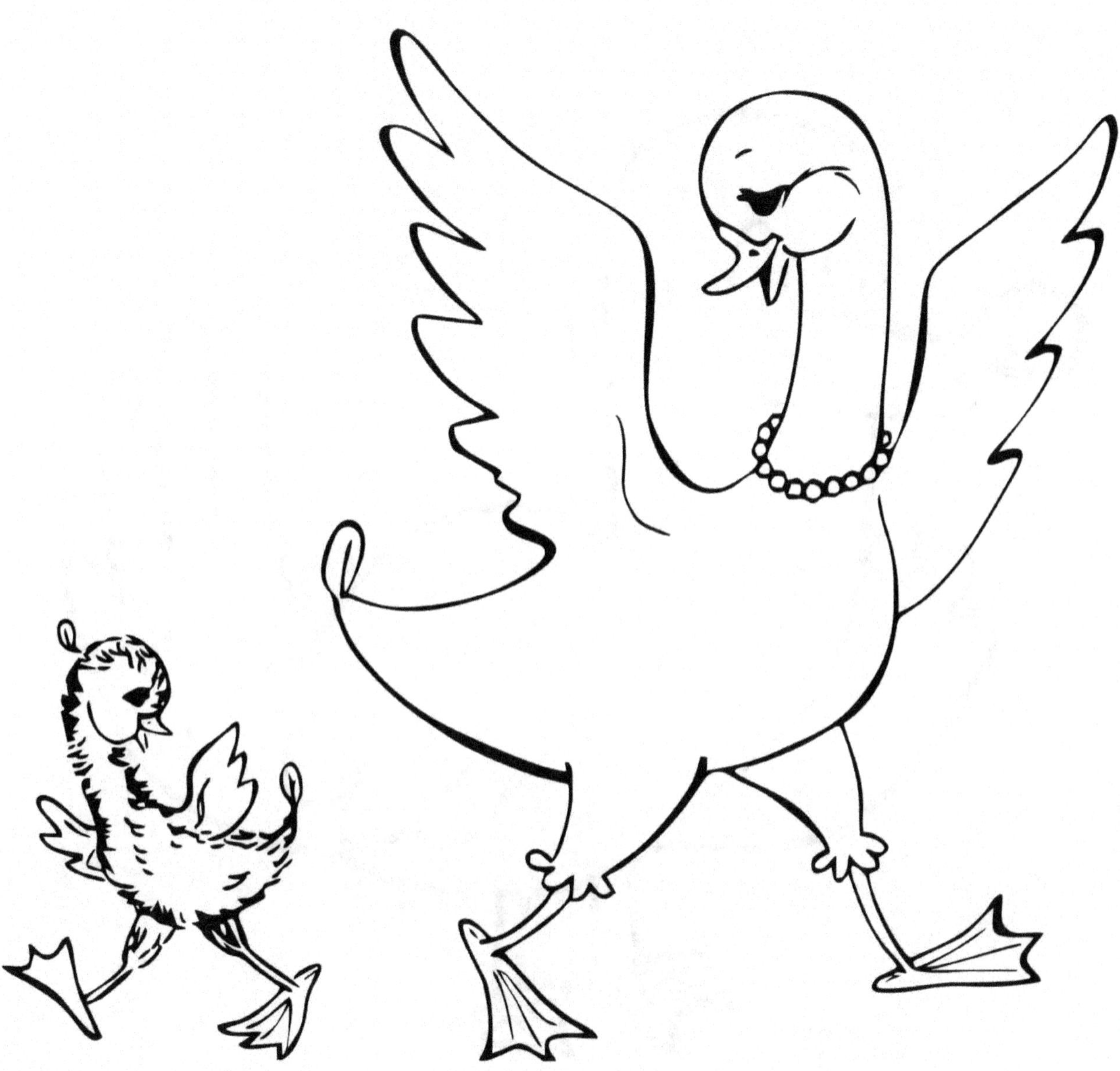

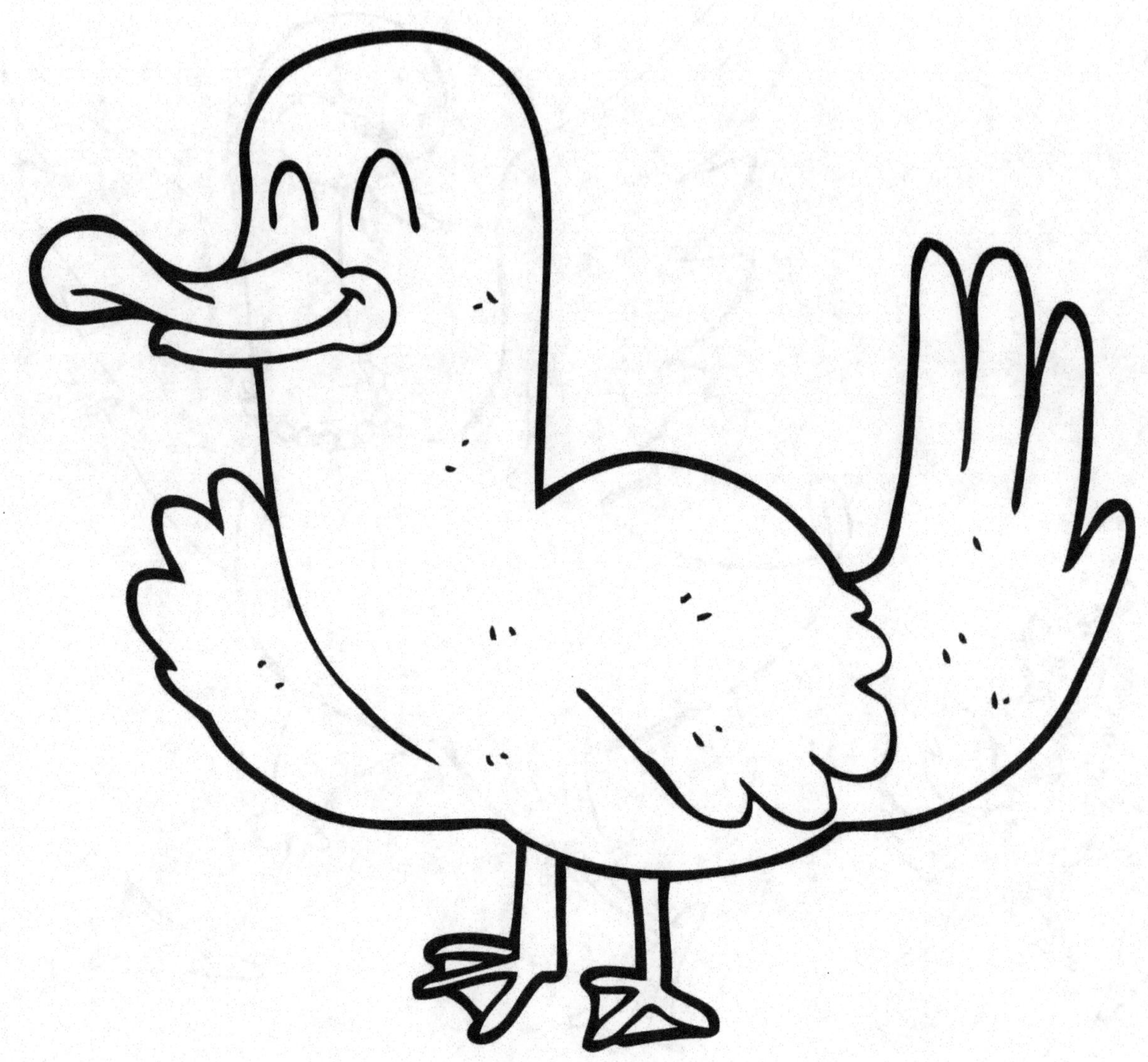

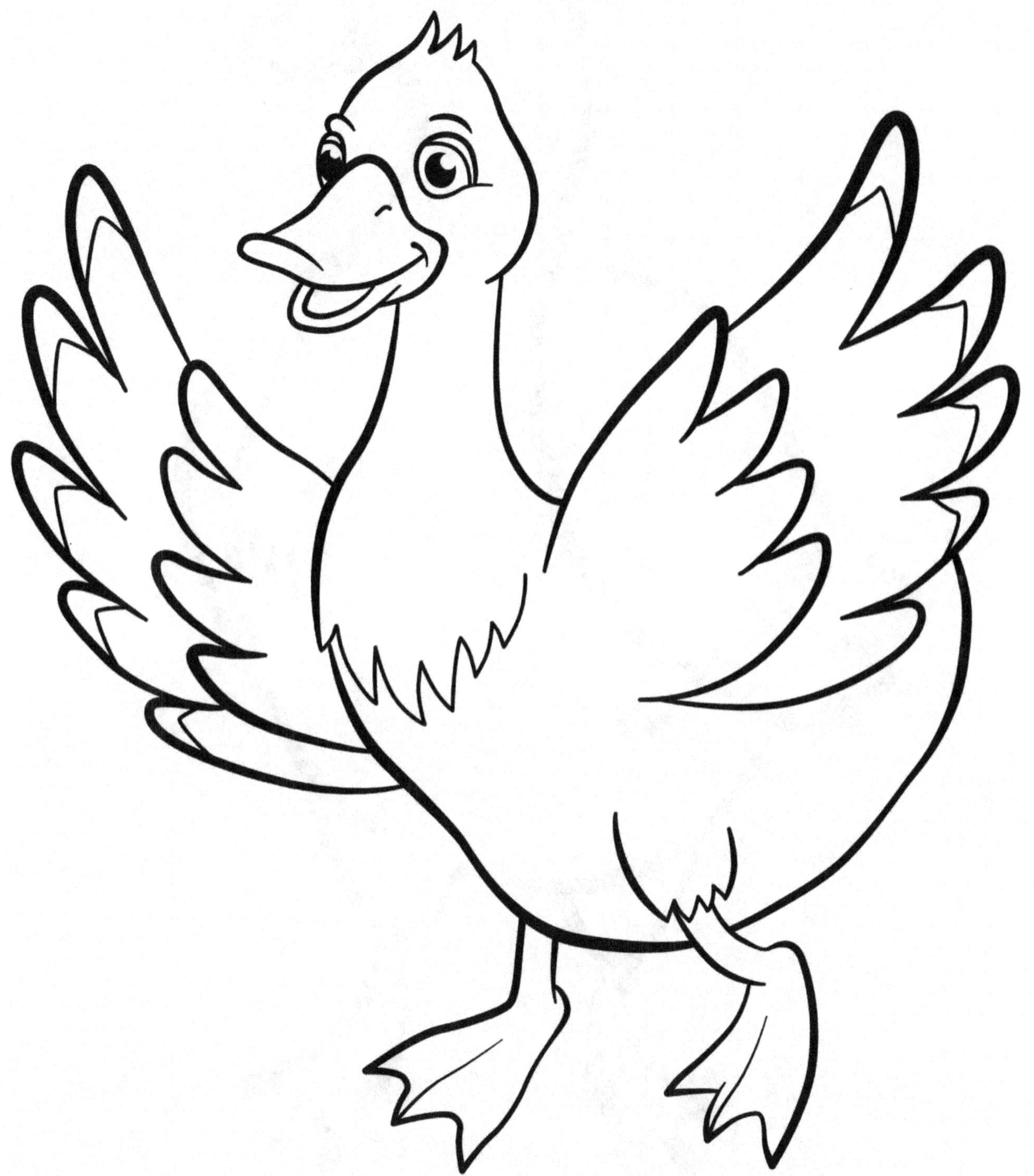

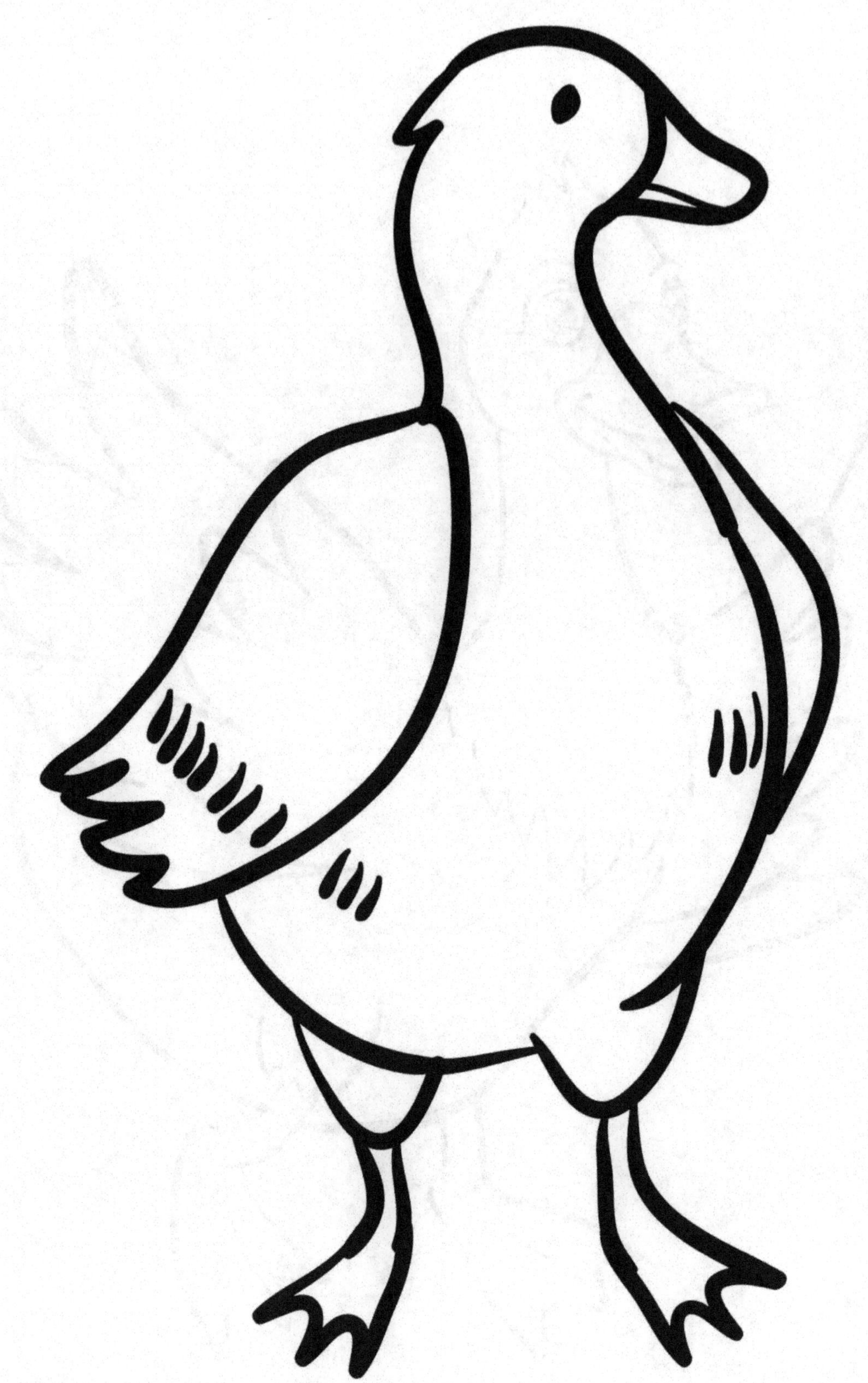

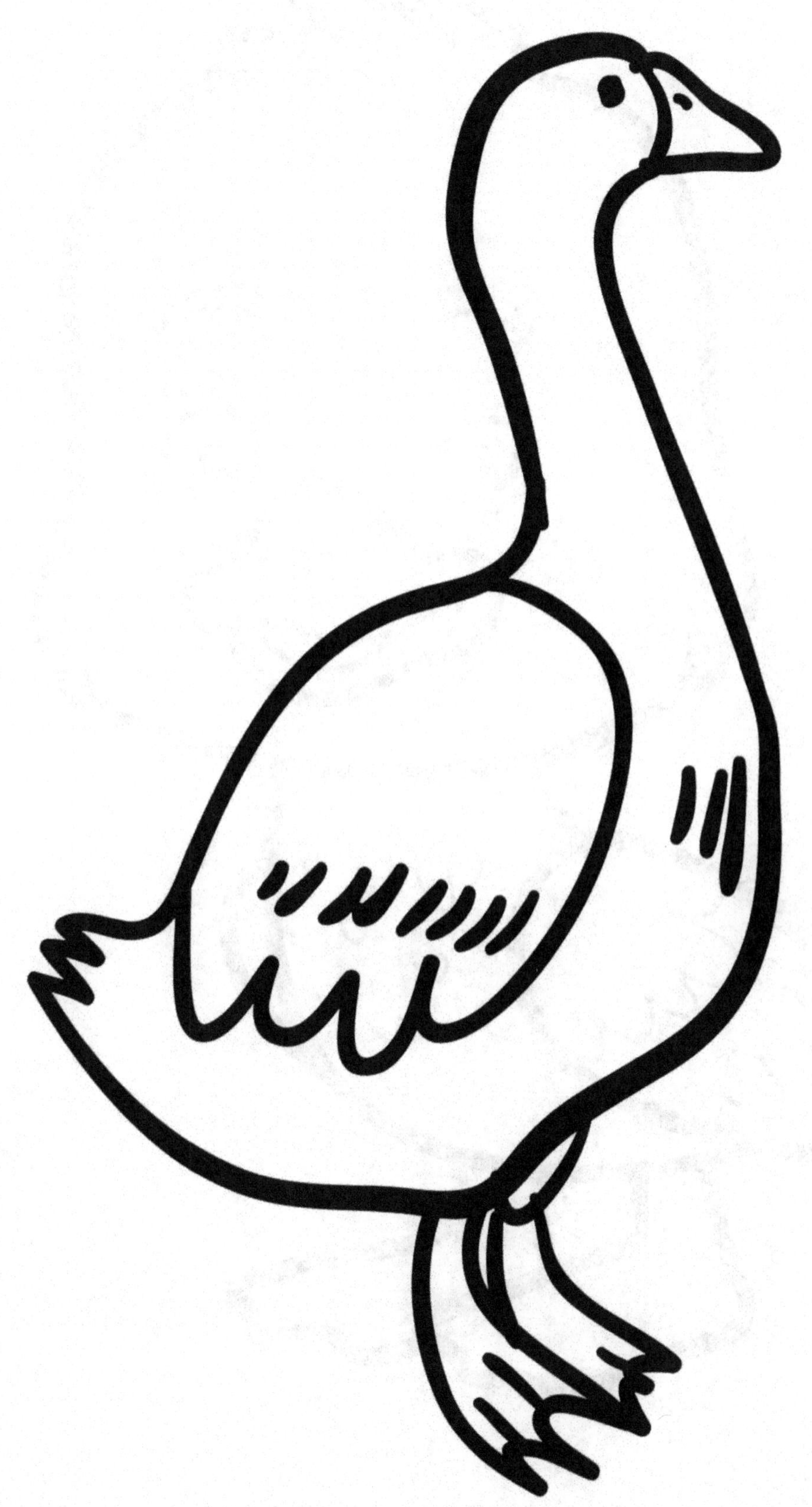

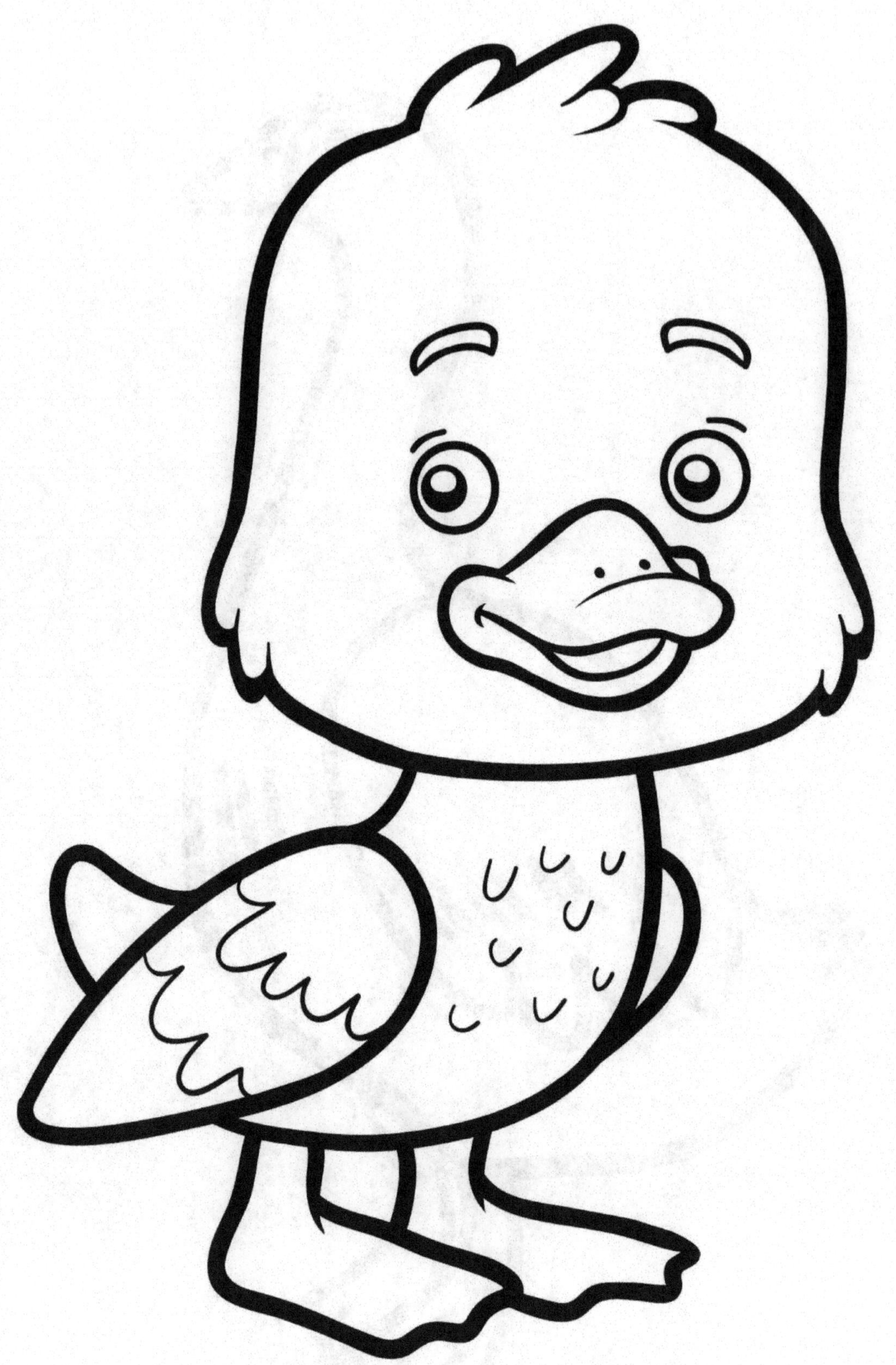

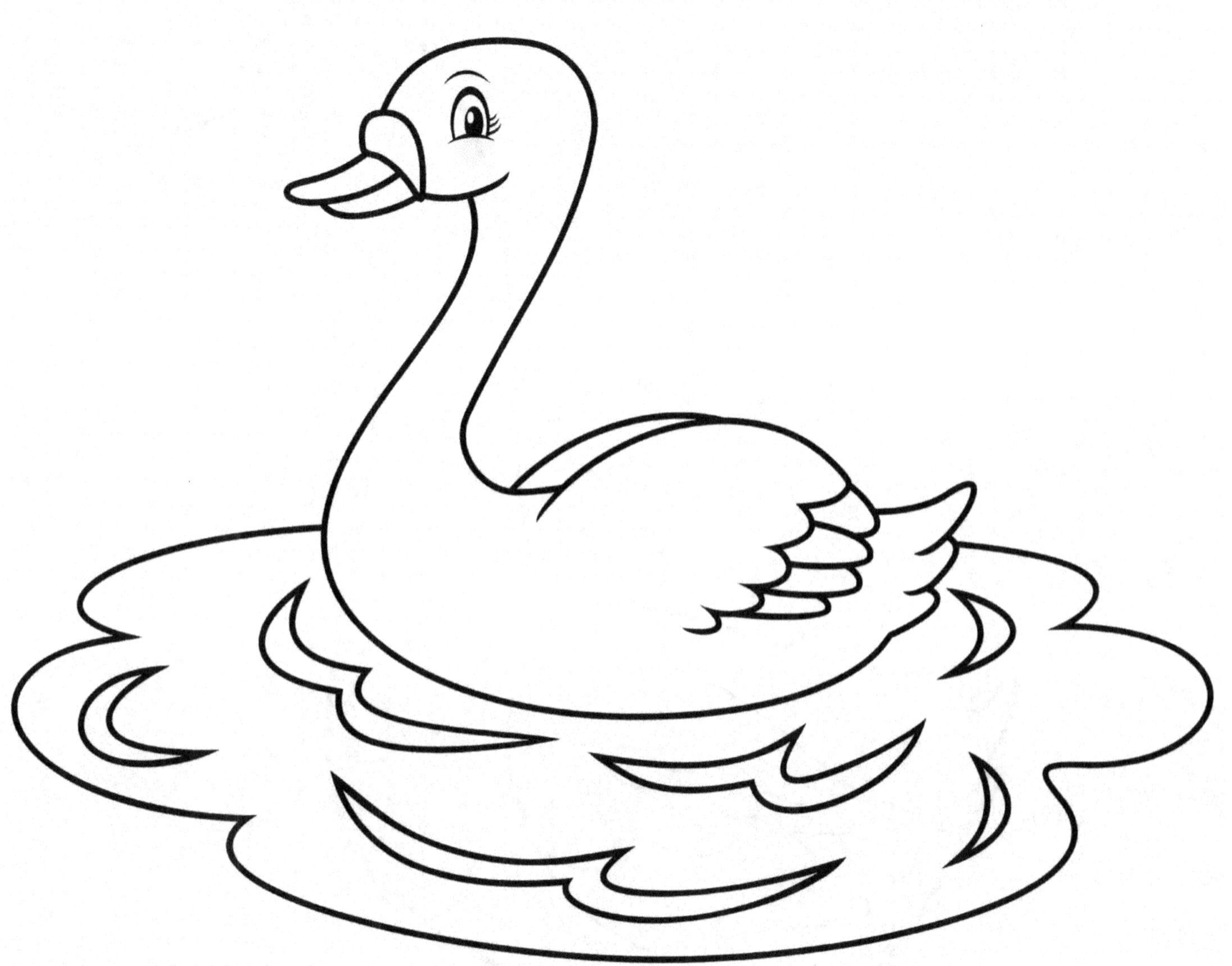

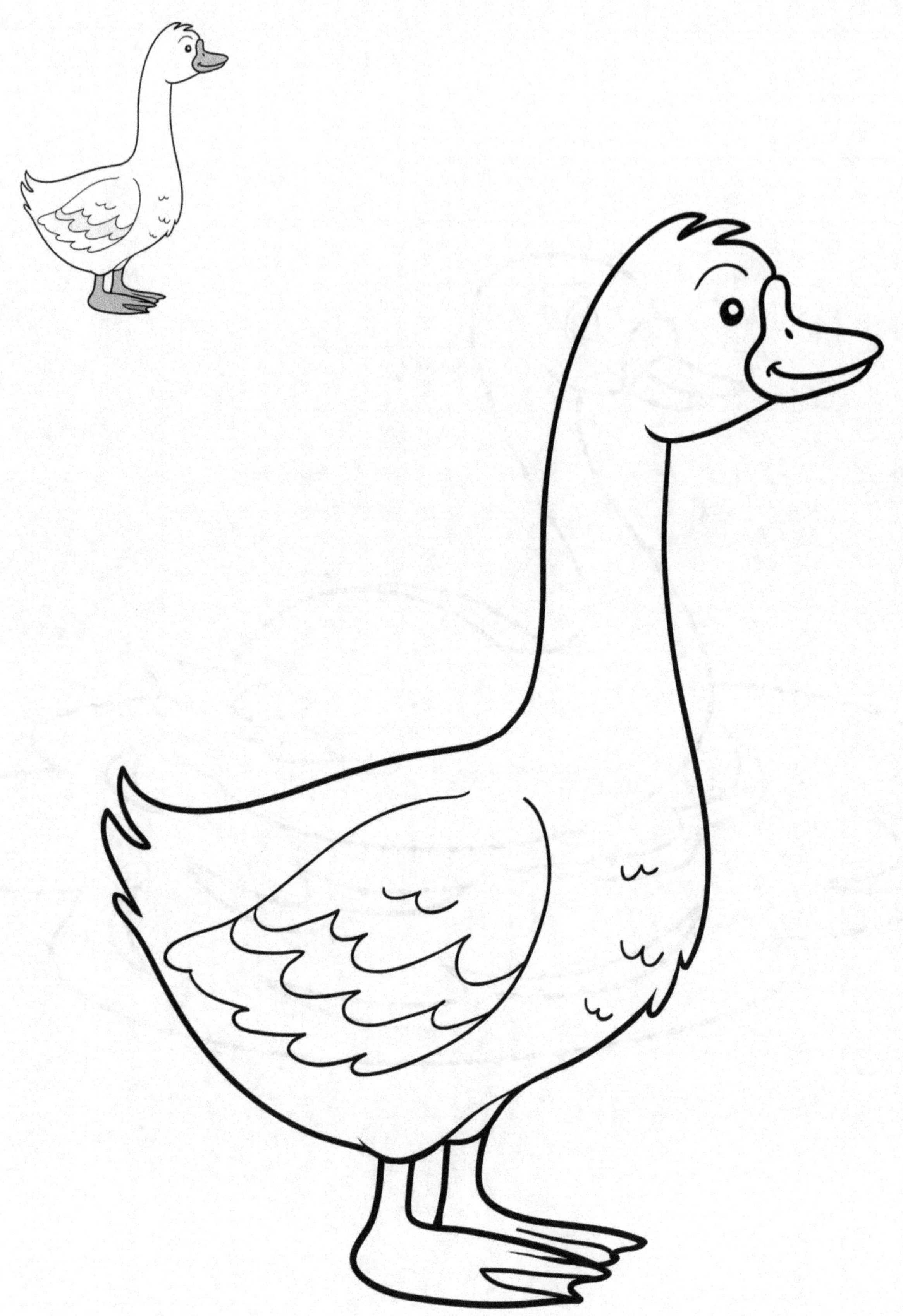